THIS BOOK BELONGS TO:

_____

Brooklyn the Explorer: African Safari
Copyright © 2020 by Roslyn D. Williams

All rights reserved. No part of this book may be used reproduced, distributed or transmitted in any form or by any means, including photocopying, recordings, or other electronic or mechanical methods, without the prior written permission of the author, except in the case of brief quotations embodied in reviews and certain other noncommercial uses permitted by copyright laws. For permission requests, contact the author by email at the address listed below.

For information contact:
Website: http://s-roseproductions.com
Email: roslyn@s-roseproductions.com

ISBN: 979-8682694167
ISBN: 978-0-578-89972-5
Published by: Southern Rose Productions, LLC
First Printing Edition: September 2020
Printed in the United States of America

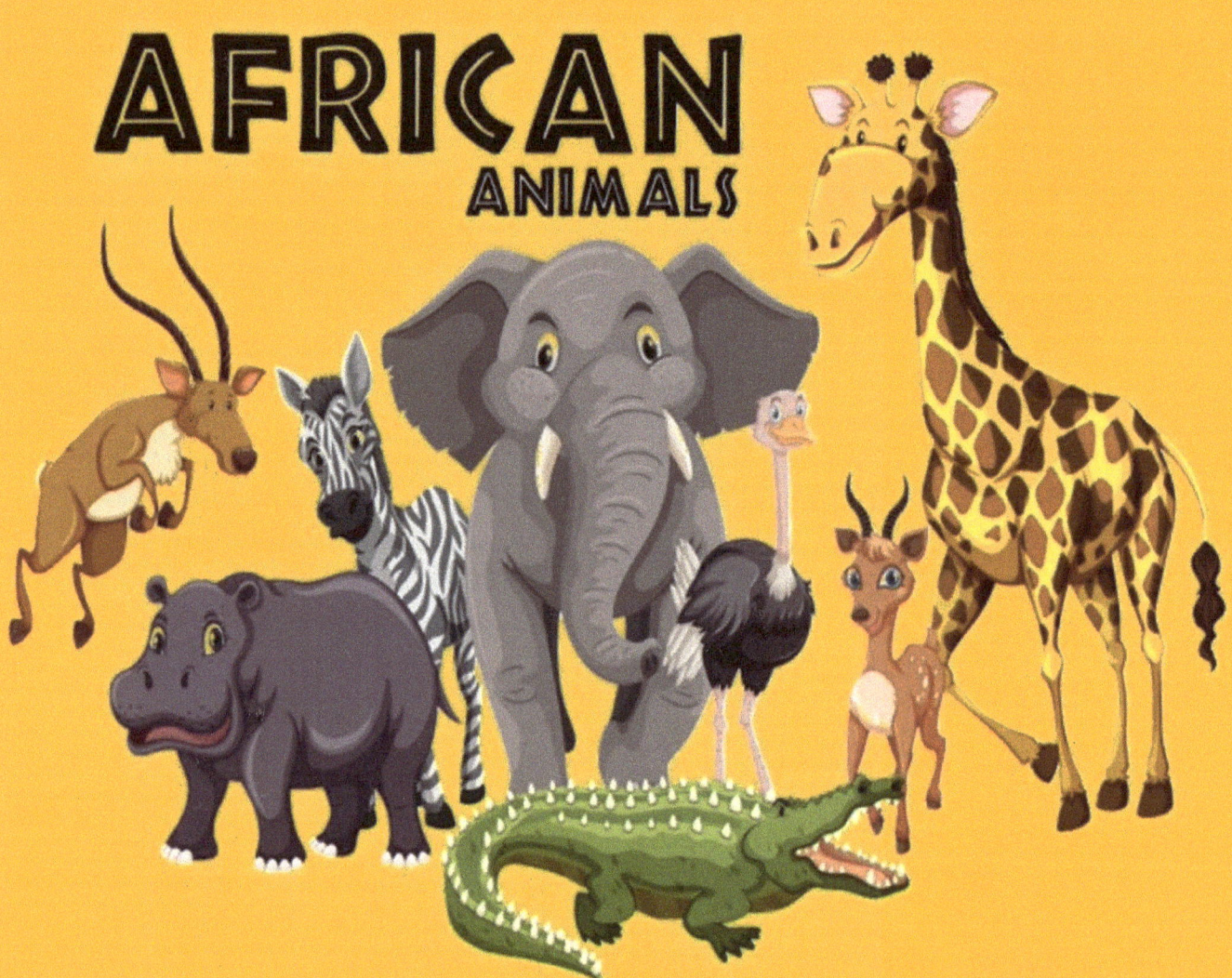

MEET MY FRIENDS

KAMILA

CHRISTIAN

Brooklyn: "I will be your tour guide as you discover some of the most amazing animals in South Africa."

Vanessa the Park Ranger will join us on the safari.

Hi, Everyone!

THE BLACK PANTHER

The Black Panther belongs to the leopard and jaguar family. This big cat is called a Black Panther because of its black fur.

THE TIGERS

The Tigers are the largest amongst the other wild cats. Tigers love to swim and play in the water.

THE FAMILY OF LIONS

The Lions are the second largest of the wild cats. Lions are the only wild cats that live in groups, which are called prides.

THE LEOPARD

The Leopards are fast wild cats. They can run at a speed up to 36mph. They spend most of their time alone and high up in the tree branches.

THE CHEETAH

Do you know how fast a cheetah can run?

The Cheetah is the fastest land animal in the world, capable of running at a speed of up to 70mph.

THE GORILLAS

The gorillas spend most of their time eating, sleeping, and grooming the other gorillas. They eat vegetables, fruits, berries, and leaves.

THE BABOON

The Baboons are large and powerful monkeys that spend most of their time on the ground, and in high places, such as cliffs to sleep.

THE GAZELLES

The Gazelles are graceful antelopes. They are really fast, running at a speed of up to 60mph.

THE WILDEBEEST

The wildebeest belongs to the antelope family. The male and female both have horns. The Wildebeest are constantly moving throughout the day and night, in search of water and grass to graze on. They can also run at a speed of up to 50mph.

THE ELEPHANTS

African Elephants are the largest land animals on earth. They spend much of their day eating on grass, leaves, bark, and fruit.

THE GIRAFFES

The Giraffes are the tallest animals on land. They have a long neck which allows them to eat the leaves and vegetation that are too high up for other animals.

THE MEERKATS

The Meerkats are small animals that live in large family groups in underground tunnels. They all work together as a team to look for food, and even take turns standing guard for their group, by standing upright on their hind legs and long tails on the top of mounds.

THE HYENAS

The Hyenas are the only animals known for laughing. They grunt, laugh, and bark to communicate with their clan members. The females lead the clan.

THE ZEBRAS

The Zebras are wild horses that have a black-and-white striped coat. They usually stay together in groups and spend most of their day eating grass, leaves, shrubs, twigs, and bark.

THE HIPPOPOTAMUS

The Hippopotamus are one of the largest and most feared animals in Africa. They spend most of their day resting in the rivers and lakes. They can spend up to 18 hours a day in the water to keep cool.

THE RHINOCEROS

The Rhinoceros also called "Rhinos" are the second-largest land animal on earth after the elephant. The Rhino can charge at you, at up to 30mph. They spend most of their day in the nearby rivers and mud holes to keep cool.

THE WARTHOGS

The Warthogs are wild members of the pig family. They use their large tusks to dig in the dirt for insects to eat.

We'll see you on the next African adventure!

READING IS AN ADVENTURE

About the Author

Roslyn Williams is a native of Alabama and currently lives in Atlanta, Georgia. She is a writer and producer, and the founder of Southern Rose Productions, LLC, an Atlanta-based film production company. Their mission is to bring inspiring stories to a multicultural audience across the globe. They are dedicated to creating, developing, and producing quality films and books that will educate, inspire, and empower. The company utilizes media and books as an effective tool for positive social change and communicating with diverse communities. She writes children's stories in hopes to inspire our children of African descent to embrace our rich African heritage and to enlighten diverse communities.

www.ingramcontent.com/pod-product-compliance
Lightning Source LLC
Chambersburg PA
CBHW061754290426
44108CB00029B/2993